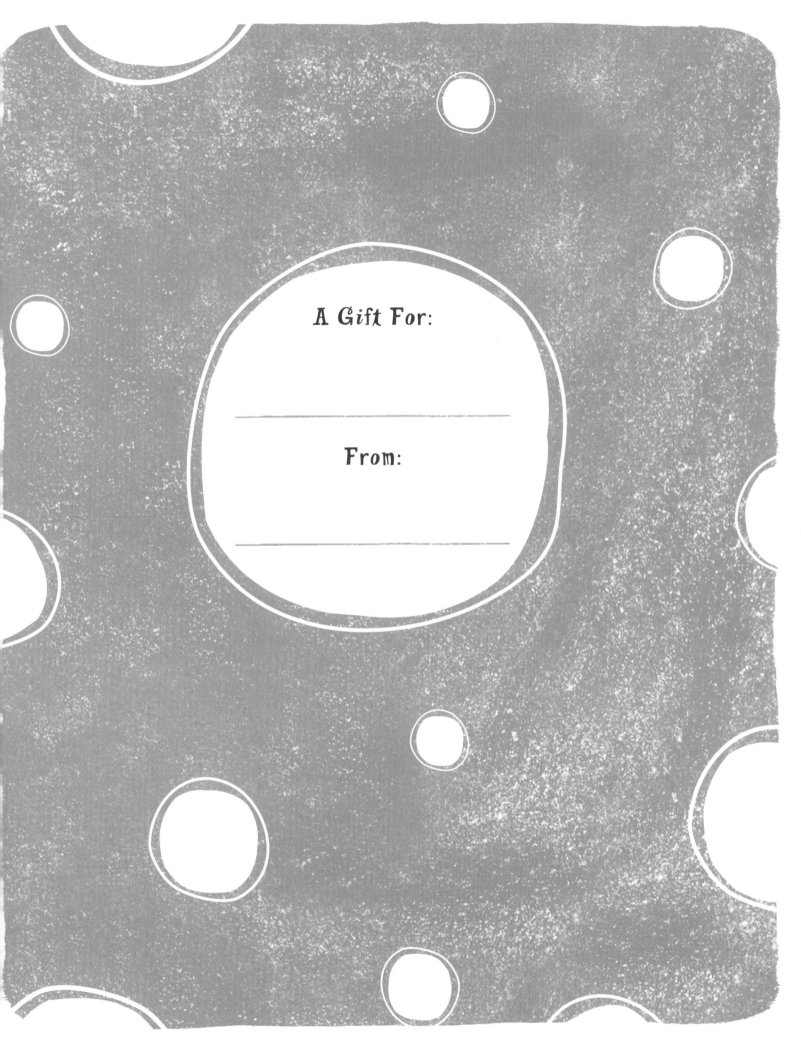

A Gift For:

_____

From:

_____

Copyright © 2010 Hallmark Licensing, LLC

Published by Hallmark Gift Books,
a division of Hallmark Cards, Inc.,
Kansas City, MO 64141
Visit us on the Web at Hallmark.com.

Editor: Megan Langford
Art Director: Kevin Swanson
Designers: Sean Branagan and Mary Eakin
Production Artist: Dan Horton

ISBN: 978-1-59530-998-3

BOK1157

Printed and bound in China
MAR12

All About
Nana & Me

The Story of Us...
to Write Together

Hallmark
GIFT BOOKS

By Mandy Jordan
Illustrated by Rie Egawa-Zbryk

To You & Your Nana,

This looks like an ordinary book, but nothing could be further from the truth! This is a superfantastic experience for Nanas and grandkids . . . a fill-in-the-blanks, draw-and-doodle, write-all-over book to complete together. It will help you share tons of fun stuff about you and help you learn a whole lot more about your Nana.

Some of it is sweet and some of it is silly, but ALL of it is fun! It makes a great project for a rainy day, a road trip, a quiet afternoon, or whenever you have some time together. There are no real rules. Whether you complete it from start to finish or tackle it a little bit at a time, you'll be sure to find something that makes you smile. And not only will you learn some amazing things, you'll have a Nana-and-me keepsake to treasure forever.

So dig in. Tell your story. And have a blast!

Full name: _____

Is there a special meaning or story behind your name?

_____

_____

List all your nicknames. (Even the silly ones!)

Baby Nana

Attach photo here.

Born on _____.
    (month)   (day)   (year)
That makes Nana _____ years old.

Set, Go!

Full name: _____

Is there a special meaning or story behind your name?

_____

_____

List all your nicknames. (Even the silly ones!)

Baby Me

Attach photo here.

I was born on _____.
                        (month)   (day)   (year)

That makes me _____ years old.

My Portrait
by Nana

Extra Fun!

Dress up in fancy clothes, hats, and accessories and pose for your portrait! Try to be as still as possible. Just how long can you hold that smile?

Portraits

Nana's Portrait
by Me

When I Was Little...

When I was little, I wanted to be a: _____

When I was little, _____

_____ hadn't been invented yet.

When I was little, I lived:
- ☐ in a house
- ☐ in an apartment
- ☐ on a farm
- ☐ in the city
- ☐ _____

It looked like this:

When I Grow Up...

When I grow up, I want to be a _____

When I grow up, there will be lots of new inventions, like:

_____

When I grow up, I want to live:

- ☐ in a house
- ☐ by the sea
- ☐ in a skyscraper
- ☐ in a foreign country
- ☐ _____

It will look like this:

Places I've lived:

_____
_____
_____

Places Nana has lived:

_____
_____
_____

Places I'd like to visit:

_____
_____
_____

Places Nana would like to visit:

_____
_____
_____

Draw your favorite place to be together!

You Been?

Color in the states you've visited. Use two different colors to compare where you and Nana have been.

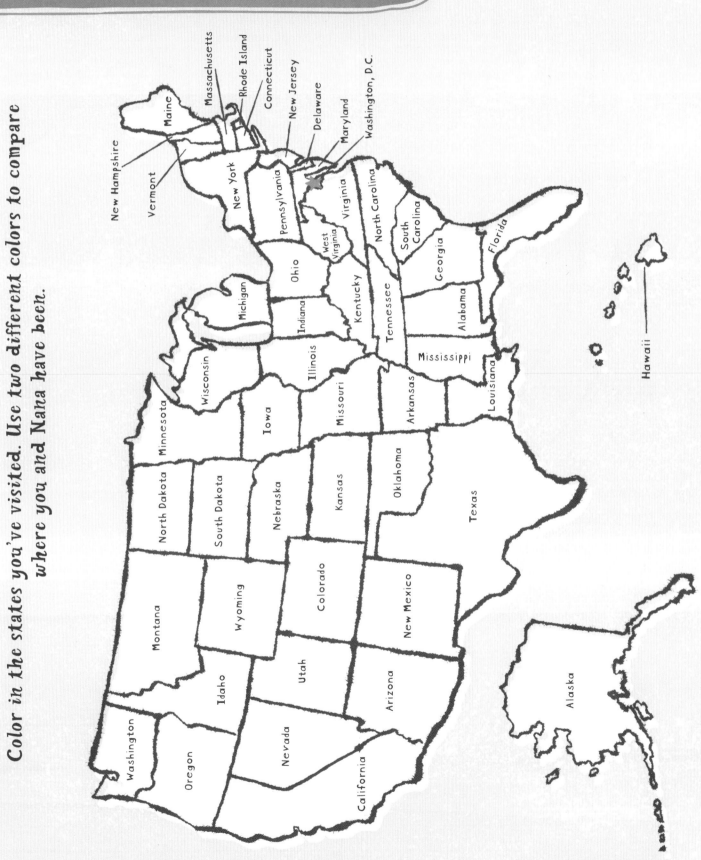

Our Family Tree

My great-grandmother

My great-grandfather

My grandmother

My mother

My father

My brothers and sisters

Me

How many branches does your family tree have? Complete this chart together, and ask your Nana to share stories about your relatives!

My great-grandmother

My great-grandfather

My grandfather

My aunts and uncles

Gather e-mail addresses for as many of your family members as you can. They'll love hearing from you!

Extra Fun!

When you were little, how did you celebrate your birthday?

_____

_____

What is your favorite holiday and why?

_____

_____

What traditions did you pass on to your family?

_____

_____

Draw or write about the best gift
you ever received.

On my birthday, I always:

☐ open presents
☐ eat cake and ice cream
☐ blow out candles
☐ make a wish
☐ _____
☐ _____

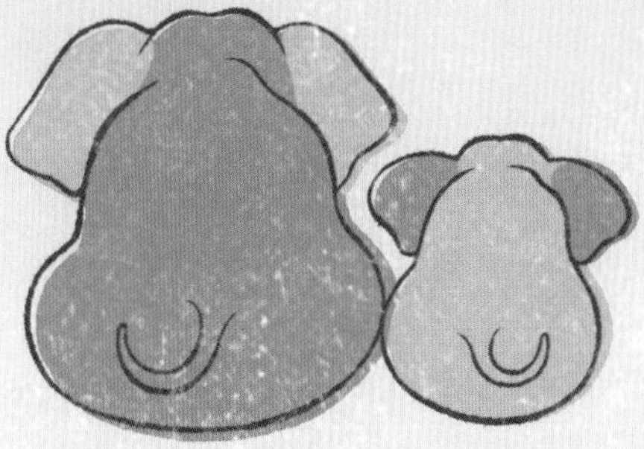

What is your favorite holiday and why?

_____

_____

Draw or write about the best gift
you ever received.

Do you have any questions you've always wanted to ask Nana?
Interview her and find out the answers!

YOU: Tell me a little bit about yourself. What have you been up to lately?

NANA:_____

_____

_____

YOU: When you were my age, what did you want to be when you grew up?

NANA:_____

_____

_____

YOU: Did you always know that you wanted to be a Nana?

NANA:_____

_____

_____

Extra Fun!

Pretend you host a TV talk show
and record or videotape your interview.
Invite family members over for a special viewing.

Now come up with some questions of your own and write them out here!

YOU: _____

_____

NANA: _____

_____

_____

YOU: _____

_____

NANA: _____

_____

_____

YOU: _____

_____

NANA: _____

_____

_____

Now it's Nana's turn to interview YOU!

NANA: Tell me a little bit about yourself. What have you been up to lately?

YOU: _____

_____

_____

NANA: What is your biggest challenge in school these days?

YOU: _____

_____

_____

NANA: When you grow up, what do you think you'd like to be?

YOU: _____

_____

_____

NANA: If you could change any household rule, what would it be?

YOU: _____

_____

_____

Now come up with some questions of your own!

NANA: _____

_____

YOU: _____

_____

_____

NANA: _____

_____

YOU: _____

_____

_____

NANA: _____

_____

YOU: _____

_____

_____

In My Own

Some really important things you taught me are:

_____

_____

You make me smile every time you:
- ☐ call me
- ☐ tell a joke
- ☐ sing a song
- ☐ _____
- ☐ _____

Three words that best describe you are:

1.

2.

3.

I like it when you help me: _____

I love the way you: _____

When I brag about you, this is what I tell people:

_____

_____

Words...

Some really important things Nana taught me are:

_____

_____

I taught Nana how to:
- ☐ check her e-mail
- ☐ play video games
- ☐ wiggle her nose
- ☐ _____
- ☐ _____

Nana makes me laugh when she:

_____

_____

I can always make Nana laugh when I:

_____

_____

Three words that best describe Nana are:

1.

2.

3.

We have a lot of fun when we:

_____

_____

_____

When Nana was a little girl, her favorite games to play were:

_____

_____

_____

A few of our favorite games to play together are:

_____

_____

_____

I have the most fun when we:
- ☐ Do arts and crafts projects
- ☐ Go out on the town
- ☐ Watch movies and relax
- ☐ _____
- ☐ _____

Time for
Tic-Tac-Toe!

Nana's Score: _____

My Score: _____

What if you were traveling far, far away and could only take three items with you? What three items would you bring?

1. _____

2. _____

3. _____

What if you could draw things and make them come to life?
What would you draw?

Extra Fun!

What if you had your very own theme song?
Make one up and sing it together.

What if you were traveling far, far away and could only take three items with you? What three items would you bring?

1. _____

2. _____

3. _____

What if you were president of the United States and Nana was your V.P.? What would be your first order of business?

_____

_____

What if you could draw things and make them come to life?
What would you draw?

What are Nana's and your favorite foods?
Draw them here:

Recipes

What is your favorite thing that Nana makes?
Write out or attach the recipe here:

Make this delicious dish together. What
holiday or special occasion is coming up that might
be the perfect occasion for your culinary creation?

Extra
Fun!

My favorite movies:

_____

_____

_____

Nana's favorite movies:

_____

_____

_____

Our favorite movies to watch together are:

_____

_____

_____

If I could be famous for something, what would it be?

_____

_____

If Nana could be famous for something, what would it be?

_____

_____

Fun!

If we made a **CD** of our favorite songs,
here is what we would put on it:

Extra Fun!

If you can, purchase the songs above
and burn a CD. Give it a really fun title
and play it at your next family party.

If I wrote a book about you, I'd call it:

_____

A book I love to read with you is:

_____

Extra Fun!

Finish these sentences to create your own "famous" quotes!

Life is just a _____.

Always remember to _____ before you
_____ !

My Motto: More _____, Less _____.

You can never have too much _____.

My mother always said "_____."

If I wrote a book about Nana, I'd call it:

_____

A book I love to read with Nana is:

_____

Finish these sentences to create your own "famous" quotes!

Life is just a _____.

Always remember to _____ before you
_____!

My Motto: More _____, Less _____.

You can never have too much _____.

My mother always said "_____."

Favorite color: _____

Favorite day of the week: _____

Favorite animal: _____

Favorite sport:
- ☐ soccer
- ☐ baseball/softball
- ☐ basketball
- ☐ kickball
- ☐ _____

Favorite activity as a kid:

_____

_____

Nana's favorite story about me:

Favorites

Favorite color: _____

Favorite day of the week: _____

Favorite animal: _____

Favorite sport:
- ☐ soccer
- ☐ baseball/softball
- ☐ basketball
- ☐ kickball
- ☐ _____

Favorite activity to do with Nana:
_____
_____

My favorite story about Nana:

Would You

Take the following quiz. As you talk about your answers,
you might just change your mind!

Nana's Quiz

Would you rather . . .

1. ☐ skydive   ☐ scuba dive

2. ☐ have X-ray vision   ☐ be invisible

3. ☐ eat one thing for the   ☐ never eat the same thing twice
   rest of your life

4. ☐ jump into a swimming pool ☐ sleep on a bed
   full of pudding   of marshmallows

5. ☐ hold a snake   ☐ let a tarantula crawl on your arm

6. ☐ live without music   ☐ live without TV

7. ☐ see into the future   ☐ have a photographic memory
                                   of the past

8. ☐ be able to breathe   ☐ be able to fly like a bird
   underwater

Rather...

My Quiz

Would you rather . . .

1. ☐ skydive   ☐ scuba dive

2. ☐ have X-ray vision   ☐ be invisible

3. ☐ eat one thing for the rest of your life   ☐ never eat the same thing twice

4. ☐ jump into a swimming pool full of pudding   ☐ sleep on a bed of marshmallows

5. ☐ hold a snake   ☐ let a tarantula crawl on your arm

6. ☐ live without music   ☐ live without TV

7. ☐ see into the future   ☐ have a photographic memory of the past

8. ☐ be able to breathe underwater   ☐ be able to fly like a bird

If Dreams

If a genie granted you three wishes, what would you wish for?

1. _____

2. _____

3. _____

If you won the lottery, what's the first thing you'd do?

_____

_____

If you could spend a day with anyone in the world,
who would you choose? Why?

_____

_____

If you could have a magical power, what would it be?
- ☐ flying
- ☐ seeing the future
- ☐ making things disappear
- ☐ being superstrong
- ☐ _____

Came True...

If a genie granted you three wishes, what would you wish for?

1. _____

2. _____

3. _____

If you won the lottery, what's the first thing you'd do?

_____

_____

If you could spend a day with anyone in the world,
who would you choose? Why?

_____

_____

If you could have a magical power, what would it be?
- ☐ flying
- ☐ seeing the future
- ☐ making things disappear
- ☐ being superstrong
- ☐ _____

From the time you wake up until the time you go to sleep . . . just think of all the things you could do! Where would you go? What would you do? Write or draw it. And make it as realistic or wacky as you want.

Nana's Perfect Day

My Perfect Day

No need to study for this pop quiz—it's all about fun! Answer these questions, then break out those red pens and start grading! Put a gold star next to all the right answers.

All About Me!

1. Am I left-handed or right-handed? _____

2. Can I roll my tongue? _____

3. Can I whistle? _____

4. What color are my eyes? _____

5. What is my favorite hobby? _____

6. Do I collect anything? If yes, what? _____

7. Do I play a musical instrument? If yes, which one(s)? _____
_____

8. What is my favorite color? _____

9. What is my favorite snack? _____

10. Do I have any allergies? If yes, to what? _____

SCORE: _____ out of 10 correct!

All About Nana!

1. Is Nana left-handed or right-handed? _____

2. Can she roll her tongue? _____

3. Can Nana whistle? _____

4. What color are her eyes? _____

5. What is Nana's favorite hobby? _____

6. Does she collect anything? If yes, what? _____

7. Does she play a musical instrument? If yes, which one(s)? _____
_____

8. What is Nana's favorite color? _____

9. What is her favorite snack? _____

10. Does Nana have any brothers or sisters? If yes, how many? _____

SCORE: _____ out of 10 correct!

Snapshots

Make it extra memorable by setting up a photo shoot for the two of you. Wear silly costumes or your fanciest clothes, but be sure to wear your smile!

If you and your Nana had fun
filling out this book,
Hallmark would love to hear from you.

Please send your comments to:
Hallmark Book Feedback
P.O. Box 419034
Mail Drop 215
Kansas City, MO 64141

Or e-mail us at:
booknotes@hallmark.com

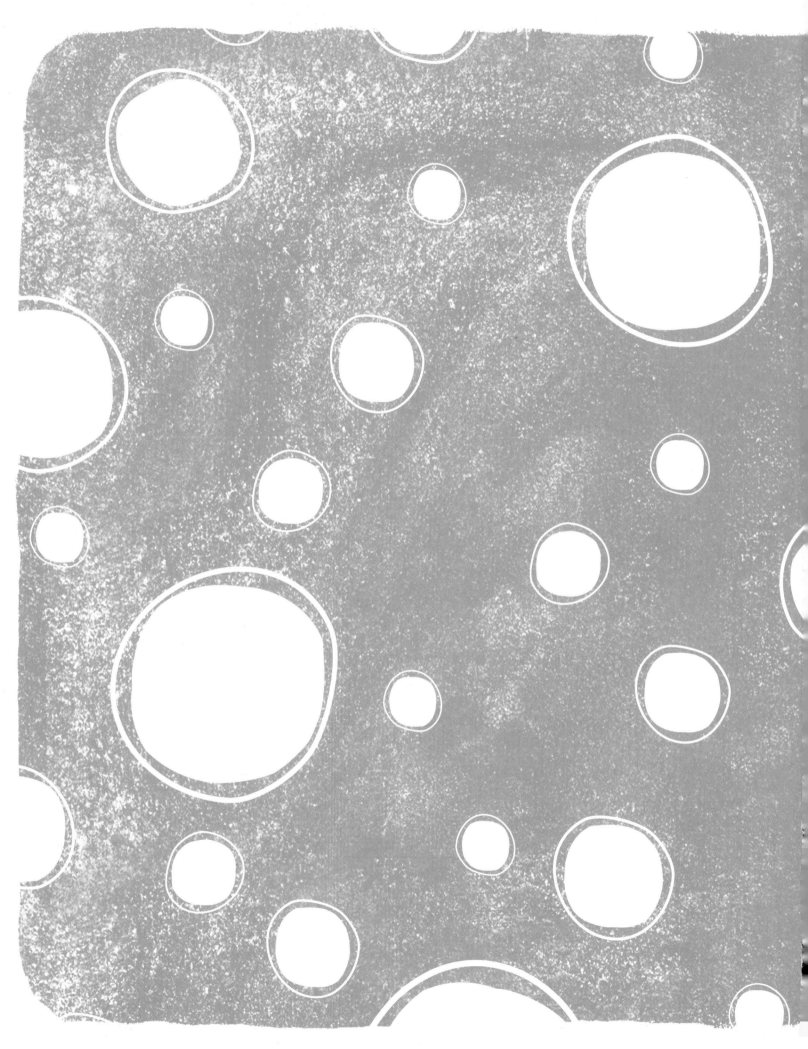